The Foothil

MW01264535

The Foothills of True Grace

Entering the Journey of God's Authentic Grace

Jeremy B. Strang

Table of Contents

To my children, never accept any form of grace that does not lead you straight to Jesus Christ and a sanctified life.

"For the grace of God has appeared, bringing salvation to all men, instructing us to deny ungodliness and worldly desires and to live sensibly, righteously and godly in the present age, looking for the blessed hope and the appearing of the glory of our great God and Savior, Christ Jesus, who gave Himself for us to redeem us from every lawless deed, and to purify for Himself a people for His own possession, zealous for good deeds."

~ Titus 2:11-14 ~

Commendations

"The title of this book "Foothills of True Grace" says it all, as we can only begin to fathom the smaller depths of such a true and amazing gift from such a divine God. Wow!!!"

– Joshua Oliva

"The subject of grace and love is the main subject that the Christian faith revolves around. I highly recommend this book by my dear Brother Jeremy Strang. I have known the Strangs for over 5 years and I know that God is using them. As you read this book I pray that you will look at grace in a different perspective. Blessings!"

– Rev Sebastian Ombima, Kenya, Africa

Mr. Strang's book is an excellent, easy to read introduction to the nature of God's grace as highlighted in key verses from the book of Titus. Jeremy expounds on each topic from scripture with numerous cross references, building comprehensive, sound, biblical arguments to the worth and effective power of God's grace. This is a book meant to encourage study and meditation of the topics presented, to spur the reader on towards delving deeper in experiencing God's grace through Christ.

– Cameron Byers

"This book reveals the biblical truth that it is not by our own works that we are saved, but by Jesus Christ's works alone!"

– Billy Witt, Author of *Sackcloth and Ashes*

Usage of this Book

The intent of this book is to awaken the professing believer, and even those outside of Christian circles, to the realities and power of God's true grace. In no way is this writing an exhaustive commentary on the subject of grace, but rather this is an attempt to direct many souls across our landscape to the very foothills of the authentic grace found in the Lord Jesus Christ. The evidences of the new birth are clear throughout the Scriptures, and so are the workings of true grace and it's affects upon the soul of the truly redeemed.[1]

The context and balance of Scripture ought never to be forgotten. We must always remember the time frame, to whom the letter was written and the totality of the writing. Therefore, I highly suggest reading the entire book of Titus, maybe even several times. I also suggest that the entirety of the Scriptures be compared as well. Often we are apt to accept only one portion of the Bible and then forget the overall balance and deeper meaning that God has left for us to keep us more centered upon Him, His Son and His Spirit. Because of such unbalance, we can become very lopsided in our doctrinal thinking and ministry outreach, thereby leading many people astray. We must believe that all of the Scriptures are inspired by God and profitable in all ways – thus sufficient and inspired.[2]

This book has been broken down into seven parts or seven days. Obviously you may choose to read this any way you wish. Scriptural references are at the back of the book for each day/chapter. This may also be beneficial for a weekly bible study, group settings or with your family.

May the Lord use this writing for His glory, the elevation of His Son, for your sanctification and in obedience to the Holy Spirit!

Introduction

In this pampered age of watered-down, flesh-driven Sunday services, multitudes are being driven towards mere verbal professions to a truncated and powerless Christianity, while salt-seasoned Christ followers are a rare commodity in this day of rapidly increasing darkness.

Accursed teachings have flooded the landscape, thus surrounding the true and biblical Gospel of Jesus Christ in an attempt to drown out the need for regeneration, repentance, and holiness in the life of the professing believer. Teachings on the true church, persecution and regeneration have seemed to be long removed in exchange for cultural relevance and focused pragmatism.[3] If the majority of churches and pastors were to biblically teach on such truths, they would need to repent for misguiding the people of God. If these things were not bad enough, the *grace* of God, another one of the great and essential truths of historical Christianity, has been robbed of its authenticity, reality, and power.

The grace which Christ authored and publically displayed for all mankind has been stripped, as if possible, from His sufferings and has been taken captive by reckless and desolate men[4] who use His Gospel as a covering to excuse their ongoing sin, thus giving a false sense of *"moral"* security. Many pastors have taken *grace* to mean, *"no offense,"* leaving them an *"out-clause"* to preach man-centered messages that are void of Christ, void of waking the dead to eternal life and full of protective self-preservations. Some pastors have used grace to run far away from repentance and regeneration leaving themselves and their congregations to linger in their sin and hold on to flesh-driven promises.

It is my prayer and hope that by the time you finish this book that whenever you hear the word, *grace*, immediately you will think upon the realities, the authenticities, the power, and the person of the Lord Jesus Christ. Furthermore, I long for you, and myself, to have a deeper desire and love for Christ, His Word and to live godly,[5] having been delivered of sin, in this present evil age.[6]

For us to be *revived* to the *true grace of God*, we must first be made *alive* by the *true grace of God*.

"Either make the tree good and its fruit good, or make the tree bad and its fruit bad, for *the tree is known by its fruit.*"

~ Matthew 12:33 ~

Day One: Appeared

"For the Grace of God has appeared..."

~ Titus 2:11 ~

*T*he Word of God became flesh, and dwelt among *us.*[1] What a powerful reality – Jesus Christ appeared and came to us, having been made manifest; the very Son of God,[2] God with us;[3] who appeared to us and with us; *grace and truth revealed through Jesus Christ; "*[4] the very One who would save us from our sins.[5] The people *have seen a great light*[6] and *as many as received Him, to them He gave the right to become children of God.*[7] For only in Him is found the way unto the One True God – *the way, the truth and the life.*[8]

He is the *bright morning star,*[9] the One whom we must *pay attention until the day dawns*[10] and He arises and is formed about in our hearts.[11] Jesus Christ, the fulfillment of the Scriptures[12] came to us from the very beginning of time.[13] He is The Only Mediator between God and mankind.[14] Upon Calvary's hill[15] Jesus was the fulfillment of Isaiah 53 and Psalm 22, having physically appeared and displayed the actual production of the grace that would be poured out for those of us who would receive Him. Oh that we would deny ourselves, pick up our cross and follow The Christ,[16] the One who became grace, authored grace, demonstrated grace and gives freely His grace.[17]

The grace of God has appeared, God's own Son, having been manifested came down from the glory of God,[18] and yet *being in the form of God, He did not count equality with God a thing to be grasped, but emptied himself by taking the form of a servant, being born in the likeness of men.*[19] We must, by faith, come to know that Christ indeed appeared. His physical appearing can be found to be true in writings apart from Scripture.[20] Therefore it is simplicity to believe His physical birth, life and death. The deeper question must be asked: Has His reality been wrought about in our life? Has the fact of His appearing actually become a manifest present reality to us today?

Unfortunately, many professing Christians have rejected the inspiration and sufficiency of the Scripture and no longer believe that Christ did indeed appear. This has had a damning affect and led to the rejection of Scripture as The authoritative truth, making the historical facts of God's testimonies of Christ and miracles of generations past nothing more than mere stories and allegories to lead to a form of *"moral goodness."* Because of this, we must be resolved to stand firm, in not only what we believe, but in what we know to be true as a result of our regeneration.[21] We must be resolved in our Christian convictions, even if we are to be persecuted.[22] Do we believe and stand upon the fact that the *Scriptures are inspired by God and profitable for teaching, for reproof, for correction, for training in righteousness, so that the man of God may be adequate, equipped for every good work?*[23]

The grace of God has appeared. Has this been impressed and embedded in you and on you to the degree that you have been radically changed in your desires, thoughts and motivations? As we move forward, we will see that the true grace of God, Christ's work and fulfillment, is honored by the Father and by the Spirit to produce a resulting affect upon the soul of the authentically redeemed. The true grace of God is the empowering point of conversion[24] and sanctification[25] in the life of a Christ follower. Christ *appeared* – whenever He is truly encountered, men are radically changed or hardened there is no middle ground on which to walk.

Have you come to experience His appearing? Has the true grace of God gripped your soul and set you upon the Rock[26] of salvation, the very cornerstone[27] of having been made a new creation in Christ?[28]

"But when the kindness of God our Savior and His love for mankind *appeared*, He saved us, not on the basis of deeds which we have done in righteousness, but according to His mercy, by the washing of regeneration and renewing by the Holy Spirit, whom He poured out upon us richly through Jesus Christ our Savior, so that being justified by His *grace* we would be made heirs according to the hope of eternal life."

~ Titus 3:4-7 ~

"...but now has been *revealed* by the *appearing* of our Savior Christ Jesus, who abolished death and brought life and immortality to light through the *gospel*..."

~ 2 Timothy 1:10 ~

Impacting Verses:

_____

_____

_____

_____

Thoughts:

_____

_____

_____

_____

_____

_____

_____

_____

_____

_____

_____

_____

_____

_____

_____

_____

Day Two: Salvation

"...bringing salvation to all men"

~ Titus 2:11 ~

Jesus Christ, the Son of God, appeared fulfilling the will of God[29] in *bringing salvation to all men.* Because God is love[30] and because *He so loved the world, He gave His only Son, that whoever believes in Him should not perish but have eternal life,*[31] Jesus Christ brought to fruition the saving grace of God and the only hope for mankind. The compelling reason Christ displayed His grace was because of the indwelling love of His Father. God knew the condition of our hearts[32] and the utter hopelessness of trying to save ourselves from His own wrath.[33] For God is just and sin demands punishment to the full.

Because of the fall of man[34] in the garden, utter depravity[35] was imputed to all mankind. Through the sin of Adam and Eve, the sin-nature flourished from generation to generation, having separated us all from direct communion with God and cut us off from the tree of life.[36] Herein contains two major truths that we must briefly address:

I. Men do not believe they are morally and eternally depraved and somehow think they can be right with God by their own means or beliefs. Therefore, they do not believe they are deserving of God's wrath.

II. *He who justifies the wicked and he who condemns the righteous, both of them alike are an abomination to the LORD.*[37]

The former describes us all. Although this is not anything new,[38] it has become very prevalent and vocal in our present age. Much of this is due directly to the fact that so few are biblically teaching the attributes of God. Because of our great lack in this area, our theology has been skewed and our minds have been shaped more by Hollywood rather than by the Word of God.

People have always thought that they are not bad and have believed in their own ideas so as to appease some *god.* Many believe they must be morally good as to appease a *karma* Buddhism type of philosophy – of course there are others who don't believe anything at all.[39] I have met professing Christians who do not believe that they have ever been totally and completely depraved, yet they cry out for Jesus to save them. Save them from what? Listen here, if we don't believe that apart from Christ we are not good[40] and that we are capable of the most heinous crimes against God and our fellow man, and that we are born *in sin*,[41] then we cannot believe that Jesus Christ makes purification for sins[42] making *many to be accounted righteous*.[43] If indeed we think this way, we must either acknowledge the truth of our condition and repent or quit calling ourselves Christians.

The second, and greater dilemma in our understanding, revolves around God being perfect, holy and just, and a God who always does what is good, right and loving. Now, how can God be just and the justifier of our sin if He hates those who justify the wicked? If He is just, the sin that was committed against Him must be punished to the full. So what is our hope? How can we be free from the law and bondage of sin and death? How can we escape the wrath and punishment of God and yet be right with Him? If God is just, payment for sin must be delivered. Read below how the Apostle Paul addresses this very issue to the church in Rome.

> "But now apart from the Law of righteousness of God has been *manifested*, being witnessed by the Law and the Prophets, even the righteousness of God through faith in Jesus Christ for all those who believe; for there is no distinction; *for all have sinned and fall short of the glory of God*, being justified as a gift by His *grace* through the redemption which is in Christ Jesus; whom God *displayed publicly* as a *propitiation* in His blood through faith. This was to *demonstrate* His righteousness, because in the forbearance of God

He passed over the sins previously committed; for the demonstration, I say, of His righteousness at the present time, *so that He would be just and the justifier of the one who has faith in Jesus.*"[44]

Jesus Christ became our propitiation.[45] This law term describes our Lord having taken on the full wrath of God, having taken on our sins and sinful nature, and yet He did not become corrupt[46] while bearing our sins upon the cross,[47] being crushed by His own Father.[48] What incredible love this is that the Son of God would be sent down from heaven, having *appearing* and *bringing salvation* to those of us who would believe.

Read John Flavel's description of God the Father talking with His Son Jesus about our wretched state in what has come to be known – *The Father's Bargain.*[49] I have included this as an example of what it took for Jesus to pay in full for our sins. It is a great analogy of Christ becoming our propitiation and how we must be careful not to complain while we are being sanctified in our own lives.[50]

"Here you may suppose the Father to say, when driving his bargain with Christ for you.

Father: My son, here is a company of poor miserable souls, that have utterly undone themselves, and now lie open to my justice! Justice demands satisfaction for them, or will satisfy itself in the eternal ruin of them: What shall be done for these souls? And thus Christ returns.

Son: O my Father, such is my love to, and pity for them, that rather than they shall perish eternally, I will be responsible for them as their Surety; bring in all thy bills, that I may see what they owe thee; Lord, bring them all in, that there may be no after-reckonings with them; at my hand shalt thou require it. I will rather choose to suffer thy wrath than they should suffer it: upon me, my Father, upon me be all their debt.

Father: But, my Son, if thou undertake for them, thou must reckon to pay the last mite, expect no abatements; if I spare them, I will not spare thee.

Son: Content, Father, let it be so; charge it all upon me, I am able to discharge it: and though it prove a kind of undoing to me, though it impoverish all my riches, empty all my treasures, (for so indeed it did, 2 Cor. 8: 9. "Though he was rich, yet for our sakes he became poor") yet I am content to undertake it.

Blush, ungrateful believers, O let shame cover your faces; judge in yourselves now, has Christ deserved that you should stand with him for trifles, that you should shrink at a few petty difficulties, and complain, this is hard, and that is harsh? O if you knew the grace of our Lord Jesus Christ in this his wonderful condescension for you, you could not do it."[51]

Oh the great love of God and the great love of the Son that He should come bringing salvation to those of us who have experienced such bountiful joy – joy paid for by His sufferings. For *there is no other name under heaven given among men by which we must be saved.*[52] Halleluiah! *For you know the grace of our Lord Jesus Christ, that though He was rich, yet for your sake He became poor, so that you by his poverty might become rich.*[53]

Although God is Sovereign,[54] and He alone draws us to Christ,[55] He still bids us to repent and believe the Gospel.[56] For it is only by the grace of God the Father through faith in Jesus Christ that salvation is brought to any man. Confess with your mouth and earnestly believe with a faith that receives His grace and receives the Christ, and you shall be saved.[57] "For the grace of God has appeared, bringing salvation for all people."[58]

"I am now talking of the invisible realities of another world, of inward religion, of the work of God upon a poor sinner's heart. I am now talking of a matter of great importance, my dear hearers; you are all concerned in it, your souls are concerned in it, your eternal salvation is concerned in it. You may be all at peace, but perhaps the devil has lulled you asleep into a carnal lethargy and security, and will endeavor to keep you there till he get you to hell, and there you will be awakened; but it will be dreadful to be awakened and find yourselves so fearfully mistaken, when the great gulf is fixed, when you will be calling to all eternity for a drop of water to cool your tongue and shall not obtain it."

- George Whitefield, *On the Method of Grace*

Impacting Verses:

_____

_____

_____

_____

Thoughts:

_____

_____

_____

_____

_____

_____

_____

_____

_____

_____

_____

_____

_____

_____

_____

_____

Day Three: Instruction

"...instructing us to deny ungodliness and worldly desires and to live sensibly, righteously and godly in the present age..."

~ Titus 2:12 ~

p until this point, most people will accept to some degree the *grace of God having appeared bringing salvation*, but now we begin to enter into deeper realities and effects of the true grace of God.

Godly instruction, a certainty of receiving the true grace of God, wages a war on the flesh-driven sin nature that we once longed to protect. This reason alone is enough to make the Gospel of Christ an offense.[59] People are willing to swallow a *cheap grace*,[60] a counterfeit grace, but when it comes to the true grace of God, people choke and gag. The seeds that were meant to be planted in good fertile soil end up being dropped along the road or in rocky places or even planted in thorny places void of real, deep growth and repentance.[61] True grace causes one to be like the grain of wheat that dies and bears much fruit.[62] To be one to receive His free grace, is to be such a one to receive His instructions in how to live and in what to deny as well.

> "Cheap grace is the grace we bestow on ourselves. Cheap grace is the preaching of forgiveness without requiring repentance, baptism without church discipline, Communion without confession... Cheap grace is grace without discipleship, grace without the cross, grace without Jesus Christ, living and incarnate."[63]

The Scriptures show time and again God's incredible glory, His attributes and His mercy towards sinful man; equally so, the Scriptures clearly describe the wretchedness of sinful man and the resulting punishments for his waywardness in rejecting the One True God. Over and over again, God instructs us through His Word shedding light unto the pathway of a right and restored relationship with Himself. It is grace, by faith, and then into a life long journey of sanctification in His grace. For those who have tasted and seen the goodness of the Lord[64] and experienced His eternal life saving manifestation of true grace, the pathway of godliness has been illuminated.

The mercy call of God's true grace does not stop at mere salvation and the escaping of punishment, but calls us forward through a life of convictions, repentance, and denial of *ungodliness and worldly desires*. Christ calls us to *deny ourselves, pick up our cross and follow Him*.[65] We are called, by His strength and His Spirit, to *put to death the deeds of the flesh*[66] and repent of using grace as an excuse to sin.[67]

Conviction of sin is an evidence of receiving the instructions of grace. No matter if our sins are sins of omission[68] or sins of commission,[69] the grace of God will instruct us in such a way that we grow in Christ. Repentance is the carrying out of God's grace in the life of a believer in turning from the sins that were once loved and turning towards the things of God. For if we say we live by grace and yet we are not instructed in holiness, we will not see the Lord.[70] Let us then *pay much closer attention to what we have heard, so that we do not drift away* from Christ.[71] *How shall we escape if we neglect so great a salvation?*[72]

God's true grace instructs us to deny ungodliness and worldly desires. This instruction does not cease with a one-time lesson or a one-time repentance, rather it is a radical change in the style of our life that begins the moment we are saved and continues the course of our life. We are called to move towards God in obedience, learning to work out our salvation,[73] not by our own means, but by the instructions of grace and renewing our minds in the Word of God, that we may discern what is the *will of God – what is good and acceptable and perfect*.[74]

Here we shift from committing sins against God that serve our flesh, to living a life *sensibly, righteously and godly in the present age*.[75] In grace we begin to long for the things of God and desire for a life of godliness. This is where many people halt in their profession of the Christian faith. Even true Christ followers often choose, maybe not always knowingly, not to go deeper into the ways of God. Sanctification for many true believers comes nearly to a stop and those who have adopted for themselves a *cheap grace* find themselves completely void of conviction, thus void of instruction and void of true grace.

> "…lay up for yourselves treasures in heaven, where neither moth nor rust destroys and where thieves do not break in and steal."[76]

But why? It is this author's opinion that many are in such a state, some due to false salvation, and some who do not like the sufferings of the flesh against sin. Grace is not the absence of future suffering, Jesus made this very clear to those who would follow after Him, but rather persecutions of various types are promised to the regenerate. Read through the promises of Christ in 2 Timothy 3:12, John 15:18, 20 and Matthew 13:20, 21. We would do well in our preaching, teaching and evangelizing to tell new converts to the Christian faith what they will have to endure if they intend to live resolved and devoted unto our Lord and Savior.

Although grace cannot be generated by man, nor can we acquire it with our works, we must be balanced as to what the true grace of God produces in the life of those He has redeemed. Take heart, there is great and exceeding joy in walking with Christ and having His instructions lead us unto godliness and away from self. Our flesh will lie to us through all kinds of fits and excuses, but run the race and keep fixed on the Author and Perfecter of our faith. It is for discipline we must endure[77] – *the grace of God appearing and instructing us to deny ungodliness and worldly desires and to live sensibly, righteously and godly in the present age.*

"Therefore,[78] since we have so great a cloud of witnesses surrounding us, let us also lay *aside every encumbrance and the sin* which so easily entangles us, and let us *run with endurance* the race that is set before us, *fixing our eyes* on Jesus, the Author and Perfecter of faith, who for the joy set before Him endured the cross, despising the shame, and has sat down at the right hand of the throne of God. For consider Him who has endured such hostility by sinners against Himself, so that you will not grow weary and lose heart."

~ Hebrews 12:1-3 ~

"I will ask the Father, and He will give you another Helper, that He may be with you forever; that is the Spirit of truth, whom *the world cannot receive, because it does not see Him or know Him,* but you know Him because He abides with you and will be in you. But the Helper, the Holy Spirit, whom the Father will send in My name, *He will teach you all things,* and bring to your remembrance all that I said to you."

~ John 14:16,17, 26 ~

Impacting Verses:

_____

_____

_____

_____

Thoughts:

_____

_____

_____

_____

_____

_____

_____

_____

_____

_____

_____

_____

_____

_____

_____

_____

Day Four: Looking

"...looking for the blessed hope and the appearing of the glory of our great God and Savior, Christ Jesus..."

~ Titus 2:13 ~

The true grace of God appeared not only for the purposes of salvation and instructing us to deny sin and live godly, but it directs our gaze solely onto God, the Author, the Displayer and the Disperser of true grace. It causes us not only to look upon the present reality of Christ in us,[79] but it points us to look towards the future return of Christ and His eternal reign and presence.[80] True grace, and the authentic Christian life, is about Him and His will, not about us and our humanistic desires to please self.

Grace results in an eager waiting[81] that thrusts our eyes, ears, desires and hope upon Him and this with a visual acuity that cannot be quenched by material or emotional substitutes. This *looking*[82] unto our Lord and Savior carries the idea of someone who is taking a motion towards a place which has already been received. This intentional *looking* is really a deep longing for *the blessed hope and the appearing of the glory of our great God and Savior, Christ Jesus*; it results from the powerfully compelling work of God's grace that not only appeared, but also motivates the heart towards godliness.

For us who have experienced Christ, we eagerly await His future appearing and vastness of glory. Christ is not a mere means to an end, but He Himself is our end to which we long to worship, to praise, and to live in a close communion with for all eternity. He is not a ticket to some thrilling event, rather He is the main eternal attraction; He is not in need of us, rather we are in deep need of Him.

I am reminded of the story in John chapter two when Jesus did not entrust Himself to those who were supposedly believing in His name. Why did He not entrust Himself to them? Were they not looking?

> "Now when He was in Jerusalem at the Passover, during the feast, many believed in His name, observing His signs which He was doing. But Jesus, on His part, was not entrusting Himself to them, for He knew all men, and because He did not need anyone to testify concerning man, for He Himself knew what was in man."[83]

So were the people looking intently upon Jesus as the Christ, with a longing desire to follow Him, be like Him, or to worship Him? No. They had no heart for such things but rather they gazed upon His signs and wonders, only believing in His name for their selfish benefit. For the regenerate heart, His presence alone causes us to praise, worship and adore Him as the central theme of our very existence. His works and gifts ought not to be the center of our gaze, our passion, nor our end desire. It's not the gifts, nor the miracles – it's The Christ, the One who is the Gospel of the grace of God, to whom we will indeed place our focus if we have truly received that which He so freely gives.

The grace of God wells up in us the desire to longingly stare into the glories of God and heavenly dwellings with Christ. Let us *remember Lot's wife*[84] as she was commanded not to look back[85] and yet did so anyway.[86] She was not looking towards the land of promised security, and certainly not towards the God who was sparing their lives, but she looked back to the land of *pride, excess of food and prosperous ease*.[87] For the Sodomites did not care for anyone in need as they entered into a life of willfully engaging sin suited to meet their own desires. And because of this, they were *removed*.[88] This is what Lot's wife wanted, her own desires met while rejecting the will of God and His glory.

We, unlike Lot's wife, need a *singleness of eye*[89] upon the Light of the world[90] so that our whole body would be full of Him. "*Servants, obey in all things your masters according to the flesh;*[91] *not with eyeservice, as menpleasers; but in singleness of heart, fearing God.*"[92] The Scriptures are clear regarding those who put their strength in the flesh; they are cursed because in doing so they turn their back on the Lord.[93] We too can fall into this very place if we live our life based on what we perceive from our heart[94] and look through fleshly eyes.

Our hope is built upon that to which we look. The very things, or persons, to which we look provides evidence to where we have placed our values. For indeed, the hope that we have will show forth its fruit, therefore let us be reminded, *a tree is known by its fruit.*[95]

Unfortunately, many today are not placing their focus where it ought to be. "*I am afraid that, as the serpent deceived Eve by his craftiness, your minds will be led astray from the simplicity and purity of devotion to Christ.*"[96] For many today have *left their first love,*[97] and many more have never truly met and experienced Christ for themselves.

Turn back this very day, maybe for the first time ever, unto the Lord of lords and King of kings. Let the true compelling grace of God bring you salvation, instruction and freedom from sin and a turning of your gaze upon Jesus Christ, the Author and Perfecter of the Christian faith.

"Why do you call me, 'Lord, Lord,' and not do what I say?"

~ Luke 6:46 ~

"If anyone loves me, he will keep my word; and my Father will love him, and We will come to him and make Our abode with him."

~ John 14:23 ~

"Nevertheless, do not rejoice in this, that the spirits are subject to you, but rejoice that your names are written in heaven."

~ Luke 10:20 ~

Impacting Verses:

_____
_____
_____
_____

Thoughts:

_____
_____
_____
_____
_____
_____
_____
_____
_____
_____
_____
_____
_____
_____
_____
_____
_____
_____

Day Five: Redeem

*"...who gave Himself for us to redeem us from every
lawless deed..."*

~ Titus 2:14 ~

Redemption,[98] what a sweet and wonderful word –
Jesus Christ redeemed us from the curse of the
law, and from every lawless deed, *by becoming a
curse for us,*[99] yet His nature was not corrupted,[100] for He
was found without sin.[101] *He bore our sin in His body on
the tree, that we might die to sin and live to righteousness.*[102]

You see, what is so wonderful about redemption is not that
we attain some heavenly place of peace, but it is that we are

delivered from our lawless deeds, our self-gratifying mindsets and the law of sin leading to eternal death; further yet, redemption sets us on an authentic walk with the Christ who enabled us the grace of redemption. His grace produces a reality of His salvation that leads us unto redemption from the grave of death and onto a pathway of purification, life, and zeal.

Our redemption, through grace, was provided to us as our sin was imputed upon Christ. As Christ was crushed upon the cross,[103] our sin was discharged upon Him and He drank the cup of the wrath of God,[104] a cup that we were due to drink, the cup we deserved. For redemption to become our very own, we must believe that Christ is our only means, hope and end by which we must be saved. We must believe that it is Christ alone who can save and we are in need of His saving. If we don't believe that we are sinners bearing original guilt (sin), then how can we believe that Christ takes away our sin?

Upon the cross Christ bore our iniquities and for the first time in all of eternity past cried out, *My God, My God, why have you forsaken Me?*, thus fulfilling Psalm 22 and snapping to attention every religious person who starred up at His marred form.[105]

The true grace of God appeared bringing a true salvation that causes our eyes to willingly gravitate, with a diligent focus onto The Christ who gave Himself for our redemption from every lawless deed. Redemption cannot be ours if the power of God does not resurrect us from the grave of our lawlessness – the very grave of sin.[106] We have *not come to a mountain that can be touched*, but rather we have *come to Mount Zion and to the city of the living God*[107] – that is of course if the true converting grace of Almighty God has be wrought about in us. As freight train flattens a penny that's lying on its' track,[108] we too ought to be radically changed deep within our very nature.

> "In these last days (He) has spoken to us in His Son, when He appointed heir of all things, through whom also He made the world. And He is the radiance of His nature, and upholds all things by the word of His power. When He had made purification of sins, He sat down at the right hand of the Majesty on high."[109]

Because of grace, we have a great high priest;[110] a perfect Savior and Redeemer; One who made us alive; having forgiven our transgressions and cancelled out the certificate of death;[111] having rescued us from the domain of darkness;[112] One who tasted death to the utmost. If the grace of our Lord be such and Christ be so true, how then shall we live? Shall we continue in sin?

"MAY IT NEVER BE! HOW SHALL WE WHO DIED TO SIN STILL LIVE IN IT?"[113]

We were formerly alienated, hostile in mind,[114] engaged in evil, and people of all sorts of iniquity. If we have experienced the redeeming grace of God, having been washed and justified by His blood, shall we not pay much closer attention to what we have heard and have been given?[115]

"For if the word spoken through angels proved
unalterable, and every transgression and
disobedience received a just penalty, how will we
escape if we neglect so great a salvation?"[116]

The true grace of God produces a powerful salvation that leads us into a lifestyle of repentance, faith and a reality of redemption from sin and a turning unto true eternal life. The eternal life God grants is not a mere verbal acquaintance with a form of some cheap grace, but a powerful demonstration of the cross of Christ that radically changes a person into a new creature; hence a true re-birth of the inwardly depraved man is made into a new creation whereby a relationship with Almighty God Himself is established.[117] It is a redeeming work that transforms from self-worship to an outward boast of singular eye sight upon God alone.[118]

If we really know the true grace of God, then we cannot continue in a lifestyle of disobedience and selfish living. Grace calls us to be on holy ground, set apart from the world and to be a peculiar people. If we resist such a call to live in His authentic grace, we show ourselves wayward of the Gospel and quite possibly unregenerate and without a sacrifice for our sins.

"For if we go on sinning willfully after receiving
the knowledge of the truth, there no longer remains
a sacrifice for sins, but a terrifying expectation of
judgment and the fury of the a fire which will
consume the adversaries."[119]

The true grace of God appeared bringing salvation and instruction through a perfect sacrifice of a Great High Priest laying down His life for a powerful and mighty redemption. The true grace of God truly redeems.

"For in the case of those who have tasted of the heavenly gift and have been made partakers of the Holy Spirit, and have tasted the good word of God and the powers of the age to come, and then have fallen away, it is impossible to renew them again to repentance, since they again crucify to themselves the Son of God and put Him to open shame."

~ Hebrews 6:4-6 ~

"O to grace how great a debtor
Daily I'm constrained to be!

Let thy goodness, like a fetter,
Bind my wandering heart to thee.

Prone to wander, Lord, I feel it,
Prone to leave the God I love;

Here's my heart, O take and seal it,
Seal it for thy courts above."

Come, Thou Fount of Every Blessing
Robert Robinson, 1735-1790

Impacting Verses:

_____

_____

_____

_____

Thoughts:

_____

_____

_____

_____

_____

_____

_____

_____

_____

_____

_____

_____

_____

_____

_____

_____

Day Six: Purify

"...and to purify for Himself a people for His own possession..."

~ Titus 2:14 ~

y this point you may be asking, *"Have I even experienced the true grace of God?"* After all, we have spoken pretty direct about the some of the realities of God's saving grace and if we introspect too long or without the balance of Scripture, even the true believer can feel discouraged. That is why our focus must stay fixed upon Christ.[120]

The Apostle Paul not only reveals a clear definition of grace's realities, and yet in the very same breath provides for us the assurances of having received His grace. Some may say, *"How can I attain His grace? I have tried and tried and I have yet to see and experience such powerful realities of God's favor."* Here lies our starting point for today: everything is about Christ, for Christ, and in Christ. If you have not yet understood, listen closely, we can do *nothing* nor work hard enough to persuade, nor contribute to, nor create the workings of grace. Grace is God's and He is the Giver. Our only response is that we would receive what He has already accomplished, and this He offers freely to all who will submit to His authority and reign.

As similarly stated in the last chapter, if we are not being made pure, day by day, week by week, and year by year, this by the power of Christ's atoning work of redeeming grace, then we stand in danger that we have never received His true grace. This may seem like an extreme statement, but let me again restate, the receiving of true grace leads one to be purified by Christ Himself. No purification – no grace, no grace – no salvation; no grace – we are not God's children. Christ purifies *for Himself a people for His own possession.* If we are to be His, we will be a pure people. Just like Lazarus, when Jesus calls us to arise from our depravity, we will awaken and our grave clothes will come off.[121]

> "When He had made purification of sins, He sat down at the right hand of the Majesty on high."[122]

This brings me to a point I feel I must urge every one of us onto further growth – that we would be more centered on Christ carrying a balanced view in the light of Scripture.

God is completely and perfectly balanced. In His grace He purifies us, yet there is a very real unknown mystery in godliness.[123] In His sovereignty and omniscience,[124] God is able to work with every one of us. Even more astonishing is the fact He can take all things and work them together for our good.[125] Only an all-powerful God can do such things. We need to rest more in Him, simply trusting that His word is true. Thereby, we need to believe His word by living our lives in accordance with what He has said. There is the unfailing love of God and the wrath of God; there is mercy and grace and there is God's justice and punishment. We simply are to live in the totality of the Scriptures. We must keep in balance the entire Word of God, not against itself, but in regards to our own profession of faith.

Examining today's passage a bit closer, we find that the Apostle Paul repeats, to a deeper degree, what he had said earlier in Titus 2:12. Remember that in verse 12 grace instructs us to *deny worldliness and selfish ambitions and instructs us to live sensibly, righteously and godly in the present age*. In the last chapter we saw how we are *redeemed* from every lawless deed, and now in this chapter, we are *purified for Christ's own possession*. In this we can see the incredible balance in the grace of God. In verse 12 we are instructed, this carrying with it a reality of obedience as a resulting effect of grace, and now in verse 14 we see that it is Christ alone, by His propitiation on the cross, that we will be redeemed and purified. On one hand, obedience through the grace of God, on the other, it's all about Christ alone, the very one giving us the ability to obey.

The true grace that *appeared bringing salvation to all men* enables us the obedience to follow His instructions in the killing of our sin and being holy as He is holy. Furthermore, the realities of true grace shows us that we are powerless to sanctify ourselves as it is Christ whom has and will do all the saving, redeeming and purifying. Do you see the very delicate balance which we live? Do you see that true godliness is a mystery? Do you see the freedom in Christ apart from the bondage of the law? Do you see the realities and assurances of true grace?

Think for a second, Christ saves people in a countless multitude of different ways, yet, only through the Lord Jesus Christ by faith can one be saved. Christ sanctifies, again in countless multitudes of situations, trainings, teachings, tragedies, and even failures, yet it is in His finished work by which all will be accomplished.

Look at the incredible balance to which we are called to walk...

- We are told to work out our salvation with fear and trembling (Philippians 2:12)
- we are told to be holy as He is holy (1 Peter 1:15; 2 Timothy 2:21)
- we are told to humble ourselves (James 4:10; 1 Peter 5:5, 6)
- we are told to repent and believe the Gospel (Mark 1:15; Acts 19:4)

- we are told to seek Him and we will find Him (Matthew 7:7, 8)
- we are told to deny ourselves, pick up our cross and follow Him (Luke 9:23)
- we are told to believe in our heart and confess with our mouths He is Lord (Romans 10:9, 10)
- we are told to stay in the simplicity and purity of devotion to Christ (2 Corinthians 11:3)
- we are told God hates those who justify the wicked (Proverbs 17:15)

and yet the Bible also says...

- we are not good in ourselves (Romans 3:12)
- we cannot come to Him unless we are drawn (John 6:44)
- we do not think as He thinks (Isaiah 55:8)
- He is the only way by which salvation, instruction, redemption and purification can occur (John 14:6)
- we must grow onto maturity taking in 'solid food' (Hebrews 5:12-14, 1 Corinthians 3:2)
- and it's God alone who justifies us, wretched sinners who do not deserve His gift of grace and do not deserve His merciful favor through which He transferred His wrath upon His Son, the wrath that was due us – whereby the fullness of grace displayed for us all.

What a perfect and incredibly balanced and mysterious path it is onto godliness – and this He left us in His word.

Aside from how God accomplishes His will and works out our continued purification in perfect balance, we are to remember the simplicity and reality that we Christians will be purified by the Savior. Furthermore, we must remember that ultimately we are purified to become a people for *His own possession*. Although this is for our ultimate good, the central reason is not for our benefit, but for Him and His will; it is so we can become bond-servants to Him and brethren with Him.

The central theme is not for our purposes and spending eternity enjoying heaven, but that Christ would be glorified, honored and worshipped above everything in all of creation. It is to Him, for Him and in Him that the very end of all matters in the Christian life is to lead us. For because of His grace, we are made privileged partakers in eternal heavenly places with Christ as our consuming passion. Thus we become bond-servants under His easy yoke and with a longing and looking *for the blessed hope and the appearing of the glory of our great God and Savior.*

Becoming His *possession* takes away the burdensome bondage to the law (chiefly because He is the fulfillment of the law). Becoming His *possession* calls for the flesh to die as He sets rightly our soul to be *zealous for good deeds*, as we will see in the next chapter.

"To merely read, study or become a scholar of the Bible to gain knowledge is one thing, but to have the Scriptures ravage the old man that still tries to live within, to break him, and to be remade by the true Gospel of grace is entirely another thing – I much prefer the latter."

- Author

Impacting Verses:

_____
_____
_____
_____

Thoughts:

_____
_____
_____
_____
_____
_____
_____
_____
_____
_____
_____
_____
_____
_____
_____
_____
_____
_____

Day Seven: Zealous

"...zealous for good deeds(works)."[126]

~ Titus 2:14 ~

With us having such a God who gives us His Son as a propitiation for our deplorable condition, shall we not be zealous to do what He has prepared for us to do? Shall we not be as a child in a candy store? Shall we not have a deep burning fire in our souls to glorify God's mighty name? Shall we not be excited to share about what Christ has done for us? How can we keep such passion inside? Have we not been born by the Spirit of God?

How are we called to such works?

"For by *grace* you have been saved through faith. And this is <u>not your own doing</u>; *it is the gift of God*, not a result of works, so that no one may boast. For we are *his workmanship, <u>created in Christ Jesus for good works</u>,* which *God prepared beforehand, <u>that we should walk in them</u>*."[127] The works that we are zealous to be doing are nothing that we can boast of as it is God who prepared them for us before we were even saved. As a matter of fact, we cannot even boast that we are zealous to do these works because it is God working through His grace, that is, Jesus Christ purifying us to be zealous for the very works that He has given to us.

For me, it is quite freeing to know that I do not have to try to start up some sort of work, ministry, etc, for I need only to be obedient to God, walking in the work He has prepared for me to do and in the power of His given zeal. In this I find great conviction as to obey is better than sacrifice.[128] If I am truly living in the true grace of God and this by faith, then my faith, ought to be marked by a zealous ambition to do His good deeds.[129] You see, because of true grace working in us, it is God working in us, *both to will and to work for His good pleasure*.[130]

If we have been re-created in Christ Jesus, then we have been *created for good works*, therefore if we be such a people who have been born again by the true grace of God, then let us do good, be rich in good works, and be a generous people who are ready to share all things.[131] Let us show ourselves to be a *model of good works*, and in our *teaching show integrity, dignity and be of sound speech that cannot be condemned.*[132] May we be a people who *stir up one another to love and good works.*[133]

Having this encouragement before us, let us take heed once again, for if we are not marked by these works that God has laid before us, and with a zealousness to do so for His honor and glory, we must then seriously consider that we have not experienced the true grace of God. Though this holds true, we must not weigh our works by looking at other people, but only in obedience to God via Scripture and His convictions upon us personally in season of life we are living.

The workings of true grace motivates us unto a zealous drive, whereby, we desire to work for God and His eternal purposes. The works that we are doing will be heavily weighed out and sifted by God as to our deep down motivation. Why do we do the things we do? Is it for personal gain? For self-employment? For attaining our salvation and right standing with God? Or is it in obedience to our God? In zeal to do His will? To be excited about our salvation and reception of His grace? What is the underlying motivations of our heart? "…each one's work will become manifest, for the Day will disclose it, because it will be revealed by fire, and the fire will test what sort of work each one has done."[134]

What motivated the Apostle Paul?

"But he said to me, 'My grace is sufficient for you, for My power is made perfect in weakness.' Therefore I will boast all the more gladly of my weaknesses, so that the power of Christ may rest upon me."[135]

Paul was given a thorn in the flesh, a pain while walking in God's grace, and the true grace of God was enough. No longer did Paul seek to flee from the pain, but embraced grace, with eyes set on Christ, so as the power of Christ would be in and upon His life.

> "But I do not account my life of any value nor as precious to myself, if only I may finish my course and the ministry that I received from the Lord Jesus, to testify to the gospel of the grace of God."[136]

Paul was radically changed from an off-centered zealous Pharisee into a man who was stripped of all earthly desires by the ravaging power of God's grace; the very same grace that was wrought about by the power of Christ Himself. Paul received his ministry from the Lord, thus propelling Him to lay His life down for the Gospel and work set before him to accomplish.

Do we have the same *grace altering* marks of salvation written upon our lives? Not that any of us are marked the same, but are we literally motivated by God's grace in such a way our eyes focus on Christ, our heart's desire heavenly things and our hands perform eternal duties?

What did the Apostle Peter say about True Grace?

At the end of Peter's first letter he says, "I have written briefly to you, exhorting and declaring that this is the *true grace of God*."[137] What is this *true grace of God* that Peter writes about?

Within the book of 1 Peter we see the exhortations and encouragements of walking in true grace. Peter describes a true grace that envelops persecutions and sufferings, holiness and sanctification, godliness and rejoicing, good stewards of God's grace and warnings that our prayers can be hindered, yet at the end he says, "I have written briefly to you, exhorting and declaring that this is the true grace of God."

Motivation of God's grace throughout the entire New Testament is NOT a life leading unto comfort,[138] ease, prosperity of the flesh, or our best life now. Instead, true grace leads us down a path of sanctification, training, persecution,[139] prayer, and a God honoring lifestyle, all while growing in great joy, rest, peace and longsuffering in Christ. Although we may not always feel these things emotionally, we are being trained and convicted in such a way that leads us in becoming more zealous for Christ and His will.

Scriptural Reminders to Ponder

As we come to the close of this chapter, I want to be sure to include a few Scriptural reminders that are good foundations for us in regards to being *zealous for good deeds*.

- "...to obey is better than sacrifice..."[140]
- "...and all our righteous deeds are like a polluted garment."[141]
- "...without faith it is impossible to please Him..."[142]
- "...whatever you do, do all to the glory of God."[143]

- "I am the vine, you are the branches; he who abides in Me and I in him, he bears much fruit, for apart from Me you can do nothing."[144]
- "Unless the LORD builds the house, they labor in vain who build it; unless the LORD guards the city, the watchman keeps awake in vain."[145]
- "…and whatever is not from faith is sin."[146]
- "Thus says the LORD, 'Heaven is My throne and the earth is My footstool. Where then is a house you could build for Me? And where is a place that I may rest? For My hand made all these things, thus all these things came into being," declares the LORD. 'But to this one I will look, to him who is humble and contrite of spirit, and who trembles at My word.'"[147]
- "Is it a fast like this which I choose, a day for a man to humble himself? Is it for bowing one's head like a reed and for spreading out sackcloth and ashes as a bed? Will you call this a fast, even an acceptable day to the LORD? Is this not the fast which I choose, to loosen the bonds of wickedness, to undo the bands of the yoke, and to let the oppressed go free and break every yoke? Is it not to divide your bread with the hungry and bring the homeless poor into the house; when you see the naked, to cover him; and not to hide yourself from your own flesh?"[148]
- "Behold, this was the guilt of your sister Sodom: she and her daughters had pride, excess of food, and prosperous ease, but did not aid the poor and needy."[149]

The realities of God's true grace are ever before us and if we have claimed to have a part in His true grace, we will stand to give an account to the authenticity of our claim and an account for what we have done with what He has given us. If we have received His grace, then we must never forget, *to whom much is given, much is required.*[150] And if we have been given such remarkable graces, then how is it we could ever boast as if we have not received it?[151]

So, let me ask, do our works bear witness that we have been born again having been sent of the Father?[152] Have we had the workings of God's power when we labor in the ministry?[153] Do we desire and attempt to do everything unto the glory of the Lord? What is our underling motivation for our works? Are we allowing God to work in us and through us or are we trying to do everything our own way, with our own knowledge and in our own timing?

"The motivation behind the things we do should never be because there is a need. Although we are called to give to the needy and serve one another out of love, it is vital to understand that the motivation behind everything we do must come from a genuine trust in the Lord and a burning desire to glorify, honor and satisfy our Abba, lest we undertake the self-seeking nature of the flesh. The proper motivation should arise from the core of our spirit out of a yearning for obedience and pure commitment to the Word of God, bearing the fruit of the Holy Spirit and not our own righteousness which is as filthy rags. Apart from faith in Christ, everything is in vain. Our works should be a bi-product of our faith, and not the initiator. For it is through that faith, and by the grace of our Heavenly Father that we are justified and sanctified in Him. That faith is a commitment bringing true pleasure to the Lord, allowing His children to partake in the eternal and abundant life that He has promised to those who commit to Him. For it is by grace that we have any hope at all!"[154]

True grace appeared bring with it genuine salvation, instructions in godliness, a casting of vision upon The Christ, authentic redemption, purification from sinfulness and a zeal to do the will of God. May we abide in Christ, in His true grace, and forever be molded into His image.

"The God who made the world and all things in it, since He is Lord of heaven and earth, does not dwell in temples made with hands; nor is He served by human hands, as though He needed anything, since He Himself gives to all *people* life and breath and all things."[155]

"According to the grace of God given to me, like a skilled master builder I laid a foundation, and someone else is building upon it. Let each one take care how he builds upon it. For no one can lay a foundation other than that which is laid, which is Jesus Christ. Now if anyone builds on the foundation with gold, silver, precious stones, wood, hay, straw — each one's work will become manifest, for the Day will disclose it, because it will be revealed by fire, and the fire will test what sort of work each one has done. If the work that anyone has built on the foundation survives, he will receive a reward. If anyone's work is burned up, he will suffer loss, though he himself will be saved, but only as through fire."[156]

Impacting Verses:

_____

_____

_____

_____

Thoughts:

_____

_____

_____

_____

_____

_____

_____

_____

_____

_____

_____

_____

_____

_____

_____

_____

Final Thoughts:

The Foothills of True Grace

This devotional is only a beginning entrance onto the journey of God's authentic grace. We have not even scratched the surface in our understanding of Jesus Christ's sufferings upon the cross, His love and true grace. Let us never think more highly of ourselves than we ought[157] and may we never stop looking into the vast and never ending expanse of our Lord and Savior Jesus Christ.

Take heed in regards to the false prophets and teachers of *cheap* grace. False prophets and false teachers will always tell you what you want to hear and do so for their fleshly benefit. They deny the totality of the Scriptures and steer far clear of convictions of sin, repentance and piety in the life of the believer. These spineless men and women of carnality deny for themselves the applications of Scripture as they are truly *"shepherds feeding themselves; waterless clouds, swept along by winds; fruitless trees in late autumn, twice dead, uprooted; wild waves of the sea, casting up the foam of their own shame; wandering stars, for whom the gloom of utter darkness has been reserved forever."*[158] Be careful to never swallow down an easy form of grace that leaves you wandering in sin, looking towards the flesh and relying upon the might of men.

"For you have been called for this purpose, since Christ also suffered for you, leaving you an example for you to follow in His steps, WHO COMMITTED NO SIN, NOR WAS ANY DECEIT FOUND IN HIS MOUTH; and while being reviled, He did not revile in return; while suffering, He uttered no threats, but kept entrusting Himself to Him who judges righteously; and He Himself bore our sins in His body on the cross, so that we might die to sin and live to righteousness; for by His wounds you were healed."[159]

"Therefore, since Christ has suffered in the flesh, arm yourselves also with the same purpose, because he who has suffered in the flesh has ceased from sin, so as to live the rest of the time in the flesh no longer for the lusts of men, but for the will of God. For the time already past is sufficient *for you* to have carried out the desire of the Gentiles, having pursued a course of sensuality, lusts, drunkenness, carousing, drinking parties and abominable idolatries. In all this, they are surprised that you do not run with *them* into the same excesses of dissipation, and they malign *you*; but they will give account to Him who is ready to judge the living and the dead. For the gospel has for this purpose been preached even to those who are dead, that though they are judged in the flesh as men, they may live in the spirit according to the will of God. The end of all things is near; therefore, be of sound judgment and sober *spirit* for the purpose of prayer."[160]

Final Thoughts

Just a few reminders for us all.

- We cannot merely trust our heart. (Jeremiah 17:9)
- We cannot rely on our thoughts – "God's thoughts are higher than our thoughts." (Isaiah 55:8)
- We cannot rely upon our verbal profession. (Matthew 7:21-23)
- We cannot rely upon our own goodness. (Romans 3:9-18)
- We do not need take any other title. (Acts 4:12; 1 Corinthians 3:1-9)
- We cannot rely our on our own commitment, our givings, our prayers, our 'Sunday' attendance, etc. For only in Christ is found "the way, the truth, the life" unto true grace and eternal life. (John 14:6)

We need:

- The grace of God.
  - o The grace that appeared
  - o The grace that brings salvation

- o The grace that instructs in the denial of ungodliness and worldly desires
- o The grace that trains us to live sensibly, righteously, and godly in this age
- o The grace that points our eyes off of self and onto Jesus Christ, authentically and with reality
- o The grace that was empowered through Christ pouring out His blood and absorbing our deserved wrath.
- o The grace that redeems us from lawless deeds, killing off our desires to do such
- o The grace that purifies and makes us dedicated unto Him alone
- o The grace that produces a true and lasting zeal for Him and His works
- We need a fire continually being fanned into increasing and everlasting intensities for the glory of God.
- We need the true grace of God, not to continually make excuses to sin against Him, but the true grace that radically changes the desires of the heart, motivates the mind and brings about new life to the eternally damned soul.

"…for the sake of the faith of God's elect and their knowledge of the truth, which accords with godliness,[161]

…share in suffering for the gospel by the power of God, who saved us and called us to a holy calling, not because of our works but because of his own purpose and grace, which he gave us in Christ Jesus before the ages began,[162]

…grow in the grace and knowledge of our Lord and Savior Jesus Christ. To Him be the glory, both now and to the day of eternity. Amen."[163]

Impacting Verses:

_____
_____
_____

_____

Thoughts:

_____
_____
_____
_____
_____
_____
_____
_____
_____
_____
_____
_____
_____
_____
_____
_____
_____
_____

𝕲𝖗𝖆𝖈𝖊:[1]

- Favor; good will; kindness; disposition to oblige another; as a grant made as an act of grace.
- Appropriately, the free unmerited love and favor of God, the spring and source of all the benefits men receive from him.
- Favorable influence of God; divine influence or the influence of the spirit, in renewing the heart and restraining from sin.
- The application of Christ's righteousness to the sinner.
- A state of reconciliation to God.

[1] Webster's 1828 Dictionary

Author Bio

Jeremy B. Strang

Christian. Husband. Father. Author.

Previous books:

Realities of a True Christian
Christ Died for His Bride, So What's Your Problem?
Christian – A Dangerous Title to Claim
Urgency to Rise – A Call to the American Church
Limiting God?
and others.

www.truegracebook.com
www.Time2Stand.com
www.jeremybstrang.com

End Notes:

_____

Introduction

[1] Ransomed; delivered from bondage, distress, penalty, liability, or from the possession of another, by paying an equivalent. Noah Websters 1828 Dictionary
[2] 2 Timothy 3:15-17
[3] Preaching should be practical for those who are new to the faith so they can understand the life applications of Scripture, but we must never remain in a place of mere application alone. We must always keep our centering on Christ and His Gospel. We must be taken to the _meat_ of Scripture (Hebrews 5:12, 13; 1 Corinthians 3:2; not the same as 1 Peter 2:2) and deeper understandings of God's character, His grace, the love of God, obedience, etc. It is God Himself, and thus mainly through His Word and Spirit, that teaches us.
[4] Not just preachers and leaders, but the masses of professing believers as a whole as well.
[5] Titus 2:12
[6] Galatians 1:4

Chapter One

[1] John 1:14
[2] Luke 1:30-35
[3] Matthew 1:23; Isaiah 7:14, 9:6,7, 8:10
[4] John 1:17
[5] Matthew 1:21
[6] Isaiah 9:2, Matthew 4:12-17(ESV)
[7] John 1:12 – context: 1:9-13
[8] John 14:6
[9] Revelation 22:16
[10] 2 Peter 1:19
[11] Galatians 4:19
[12] Matthew 5:17-20
[13] John 1:1-5
[14] 1 Timothy 2:5
[15] Luke 23:33(KJV)
[16] Luke 9:23
[17] Romans 5:15-17
[18] John 1:1, 14
[19] Philippians 2:6-7
[20] See *The Antiquities of the Jews*, Book 18, Chapter 3 by Titus Flavius Josephus
[21] *In theology, new birth by the grace of God; that change by which the will and natural enmity of man to God and his law are subdued, and a principle of supreme love to God and his law, or holy affections, are implanted in the heart.* Noah Webster's 1828 Dictionary
[22] 2 Timothy 3:12
[23] 2 Timothy 3:16, 17 – also see 2 Peter 1:20,21
[24] *In a theological or moral sense, a change of heart, or dispositions, in which the enmity of the heart to God and his law and the obstinacy of the will are subdued, and are succeeded by supreme love to God and his moral government, and a reformation of life.* Noah Webster's 1828 Dictionary
[25] *The act of making holy. In an evangelical sense, the act of*

God's grace by which the affections of men are purified or alienated from sin and the world, and exalted to a supreme love to God. Noah Webster's 1828 Dictionary

[26] Psalm 40:2; Matthew 16:18

[27] Matthew 21:42; Mark 12:10; Luke 20:17; Acts 4:11

[28] 2 Corinthians 5:17; Galatians 6:15

Chapter Two

[29] Hebrews 10:7; Luke 22:42; Matthew 6:10

[30] 1 John 4:16

[31] John 3:16

[32] Genesis 6:5, 8:21

[33] John 3:36

[34] Genesis 3

[35] Corruption; a vitiated state; A vitiated state of heart; wickedness. Noah Websters 1828 Dictionary

[36] Genesis 3:24

[37] Proverbs 17:15

[38] Ecclesiastes 1:9

[39] One report recently revealed there are over 40,000 registered denominations under the label *"Christian"* alone. This is not to mention multi-millions of different beliefs and *gods* in the world.

[40] Romans 3:23 (9-26)

[41] Psalm 51:5

[42] Hebrews 1:3

[43] Isaiah 53:11

[44] Romans 3:21-26

[45] The act of appeasing wrath and conciliating the favor of an offended person. Noah Websters 1828 Dictionary

[46] Acts 2:31, 13:35

[47] 1 Peter 2:24

[48] Isaiah 53:10

[49] Although God does not bargain for anything, the example that Flavel beautifully portrays is that Christ had to suffer to

[50] I highly recommend reading 1 Peter 2:21-25

[51] *Opens the Covenant of Redemption betwixt the Father and the Redeemer; The Father's Bargain* – Volume 1, Sermon 3 – John Flavel

[52] Acts 4:12

[53] 2 Corinthians 8:9

[54] Supreme power or authority

[55] John 6:44

[56] Mark 1:15, Acts 19:4

[57] Romans 10:9, 10

[58] Titus 2:11; ESV

Chapter Three

[59] Romans 9:33; Isaiah 28:16; 1 Peter 2:8

[60] *Cheap grace* – A term first brought to light by Dietrich Bonhoeffer, *The Cost of Discipleship*. My usage here relates to a broader context, not just the removal of Christ and the cross in salvation by grace alone, but includes the justification of willful and ongoing sin by using grace as the means to continue in such sin. Also see author's previous book, *Realities of a True Christian*, chapter 11, *Realities of True Grace*, for more information.

[61] Matthew 13:3-9, 18-23

[62] John 12:24, 25

[63] Dietrich Bonhoeffer, *The Cost of Discipleship*

[64] Psalm 34:8

[65] Luke 9:23, 14:27; Matthew 10:28, 39

[66] Romans 8:13 – context verses 1-17; John Owen's book, *The Mortification of Sin*, is a good help on 8:13.

[67] Romans 6:1-4

[68] Neglect or failure to do something which a person had power to do, or which duty required to be. Noah Websters 1828 Dictionary

[69] The act of committing, doing, performing, or perpetrating; as the commission of a crime. Noah Websters 1828

Dictionary
[70] Hebrews 12:14
[71] Hebrews 2:1 – context 1:1-2:4
[72] Hebrews 2:3
[73] Philippians 2:12
[74] Romans 12:1-2 ESV
[75] Also see, Galatians 5:16, 17, 6:8
[76] Matthew 6:20
[77] Hebrews 12:7
[78] Read all of Hebrews 11 as well.

Chapter Four

[79] John 14:18-21
[80] Revelation 19:11-21
[81] As the ESV uses *waiting* instead of looking in Titus 2:13
[82] *looking* – prosdechomai(4327); taken from pros(4314) & dechamai(1209); to receive to oneself; accepted, accepting, cherish, looking for, receive, receives, waiting anxiously for, waiting for. Taken from the New American Standard Exhaustive Concordance of the Bible; copyright © 1981 The Lockman Foundation, LaHabra, California; Based on the Strong's numbering system.
[83] John 2:23-25
[84] Luke 17:32
[85] Genesis 19:17
[86] Genesis 19:26
[87] Ezekiel 16:49
[88] Ezekiel 16:50
[89] Matthew 6:22
[90] John 8:12, 1:9, 9:5, 12:46; Luke 11:34
[91] *flesh* – used here not relating to sin, but to the physical body in the physical world
[92] Colossians 3:22 KJV
[93] Jeremiah 17:5

[94] Jeremiah 17:9
[95] Matthew 12:33; Luke 6:44
[96] 2 Corinthians 11:3
[97] Revelation 2:4

Chapter Five

[98] Repurchase of captured goods or prisoners; the act of procuring the deliverance of persons or things from the possession and power of captors by the payment of an equivalent; ransom; release; as the redemption of prisoners taken in war; the redemption of a ship and cargo. Noah Websters 1828 Dictionary
[99] Galatians 3:13
[100] Acts 2:31, 13:34-37
[101] 1 Peter 2:22
[102] 1 Peter 2:24
[103] Isaiah 53:10
[104] Matthew 26:39(36-96); John 18:11; Luke 22:42
[105] Isaiah 52:13-53:12
[106] 1 John 3:4
[107] Hebrews 12:18-24
[108] Why do I use such an analogy? Simply to give strong emphasis and pose the thought, which is bigger and more powerful, the Everlasting God, or a freight train? How can we be saved and yet not radically changed by our Great God? (Thought owed to Paul Washer)
[109] Hebrews 1:1-3
[110] Hebrews 4:14-16
[111] Colossians 2:13, 14
[112] Colossians 1:13
[113] Romans 6:1, 2
[114] Colossians 1:21, 22
[115] Hebrews 2:1
[116] Hebrews 2:2, 3
[117] John 17:3
[118] Jeremiah 9:23-25

[119] Hebrews 10:26, 27 (context 26-31)

Chapter Six

[120] Hebrews 12:2
[121] John 11:43, 44
[122] Hebrews 1:3
[123] 1 Timothy 3:16
[124] *infinite knowledge*
[125] Romans 8:28-29
[126] English Standard Version (ESV) - *works*
[127] Ephesians 2:8-10 (ESV)
[128] 1 Samuel 15:22
[129] James 2:18
[130] Philippians 2:13
[131] 1 Timothy 6:18
[132] Titus 2:7, 8 (ESV)
[133] Hebrews 10:24
[134] 1 Corinthians 3:13 (ESV)
[135] 2 Corinthians 12:9(ESV) context vs. 7-10
[136] Acts 20:24 (ESV)
[137] 1 Peter 5:12 (ESV)
[138] Comfort here meaning comforts of worldliness
[139] Of various sorts
[140] 1 Samuel 15:22
[141] Isaiah 64:6 (ESV)
[142] Hebrews 11:6
[143] 1 Corinthians 10:31
[144] John 15:5
[145] Psalm 127:1
[146] Romans 14:23
[147] Isaiah 66:1, 2
[148] Isaiah 58:5-7
[149] Ezekiel 16:49
[150] Luke 12:48
[151] 1 Corinthians 4:7
[152] John 5:36

153 Ephesians 3:7
154 Brother Joshua Oliva
155 Acts 17:24, 25
156 1 Corinthians 3:10-15

Final Thoughts: The Foothills of True Grace

157 Romans 12:3
158 Jude 12, 13
159 1 Peter 2:21-24
160 1 Peter 4:1-7
161 Titus 1:1 (ESV)
162 2 Timothy 1:8, 9 (ESV)
163 2 Peter 3:18

Made in the USA
Charleston, SC
07 March 2015